Cornw[...]
SHIPWR[...]

GW00644996

South Coast

Medieval print c1400, of a ship sinking. The two mystery objects at the top may be missiles, suggesting the ship has been fired on from land.

For further information of all the titles in this series please visit:-
www.tormark.co.uk

First published 2009 by Tor Mark, United Downs Ind Est, Redruth,
Cornwall TR16 5HY

ISBN 978 085025 414 3

Acknowledgements

Front cover: *Bay of Panama* (Gibsons of Scilly)
This page *Brankelow* (Richard Larn Collection)
Back cover: www.aqua-photography.com – photo by K J Hunkin
All other pictures acknowledged under image

Printed by R Booth Ltd, The Praze, Penryn, Cornwall TR10 8AA

Cornwall, shipwrecks and smuggling are synonymous, which is hardly surprising considering it has the longest coastline of any county in the British Isles. Its south coast facing the English Channel has witnessed the passage of a millennia of vessels from across the world destined for London and the continent.

The south coast has claimed over 2,500 wrecks, which continues to grow as documentary research and diving finds evidence of additional long forgotten ships. In searching for one documentary source which best illustrates this huge, tragic and often forgotten loss of life, ships and cargo, our attention was drawn to the Penheleg Manuscript. This was discovered by P.A. Pool in 1955, purchased in 1958 and now safely deposited in the County Record Office at Truro. Written in 1580 by John Penheleg, Bailiff of the Hundred of Penwith, covering Penzance and the extreme western part of Cornwall, it is a record of events from 1530 to 1580. It includes the sworn testimony of many old men under the heading,

Here followeth wracks of the Sea,

from which these are examples chosen at random:

Wrack the 6th (year) of Henry VIII – Pers John of the age of 75 sworn at the court aforesaid, that he did see a ship which came to land wracked in Mount's Bay between Pensance and Markatowe and there was in this ship much spices and fine linen cloths and clothes so floated along the strand upon divers gentlemens' lands.

Wrack ye 7th Henry VIII. – Stephen Powlye of the age of 90 sworn before William Gilbert of the Franchis holden at Pensance the 22nd February Anno 7th Eliz, saith that he had seen 7 ships and barks lost between Lelant water and St.Ives loaden with divers wares as iron pans and cloth and other wares.

Triall of Wrack anno 22nd Henry VIII – Harry Angwyne of the age of 76 sworn at the Court that he did see one hulk ship lost at Senar Clyff loaden with salt and the men all drowned. Sir John Arundell's officers parted the wreck with the finders and gave them half for their pains and the other half they carried away.

Anno 9th & 10th Eliz. One ship lost at Long Shipps in the Lands End; one hogshead of nutmegs found at Polpyre in St. Juste; one chest full of cinnamion and cloves found upon the sands of Meen; found at Polpyre another one hogshead of nutmegs.

Anno 13th Eliz. One hulk ship found within the key of Pensance the burden of a 100 tuns having all her masts cables anchors and sailes and all manner of tackles and ropes appertaining with quarter slings and 6 double basses (bronze guns) *which ship John Penheleg the Head Bayliff then did enter into the same ship and kept the same to Sir John Arundell's use as Lord of the Franchise because the owner and master thereof died and no man came to lay any claim to the same; the ship was out of Lebeck.*

The earliest newspaper accounts of shipwreck in Cornwall appeared in Felix Farley's *Bristol Journal* from 1714, and

Trewman's Exeter Flying Post commencing 1763, from which the following are just two typical entries:

St. Mary's Island, Scilly: For Sale on Thursday the 8th day of July next 1784, by public auction at the house of Mr William Edwards by 2 o'clock in the afternoon, the hull of the ship Sophia, burthen about 350 tons, lately stranded there in her passage from Wyberg to Liverpool and now lying on St.Mary's beach.

Advertisement: Dutch ship Ganges, J.F.Shultz late master, from Middelburgh to the East indies; whereas large quantities of dollars and other silver coins have been plundered out of this ship, any person or persons who have bought any of the same or have any in their custody are hereby required immediately to give an account thereof to Timothy Nucelle, London Agent.

This booklet is an account of but a relatively small number of shipwrecks along the south coast, considering the overall total around Cornwall and Scilly. Many are obscure, others less so, but all are historic and part of Cornwall's maritime legacy for differing reasons. Many of the accounts have the personal touch of the authors, where they have been involved in their location, survey, exploration or salvage during a lifetime of wreck diving. Their extensive research continues in libraries, museums, institutions, public repositories and private collections not only in Cornwall and Devon, but London and elsewhere.

RICHARD & BRIDGET LARN
St Mary's, Isles of Scilly 2008

St Anthony

19 January 1526 - Gunwalloe Fishing Cove

When in 1526 news from Gunwalloe on the Lizard Peninsula reached nearby Breage, Mullion and Helston that a large Portuguese carrack was ashore only a short distance from the beach, as many as could get away from their work took to the Lizard Road, heading for the east end of Loe Bar. Here they met with other Cornishmen, women and children all armed with 'wrecking' tools, either crowbars, axes, lengths of rope, sacks or wheel barrows, until literally hundreds of people thronged the foreshore. The same questions were on everyone's lips, 'What ship was it, where has it come from?' But more importantly, 'What was she carrying?' Was it something worth plundering, or merely a mundane but still worthwhile cargo of turnips, coal or wood? The word quickly spread that she was in fact the carrack *St Anthony*, a personal ship of King John III of Portugal, carrying a crew of 86, half of whom had drowned trying to reach the shore. According to her captain, Diogo Vaz and other Portuguese gentleman who had reached the safety of the beach, she carried an absolute fortune in gold, silver, jewels, copper, musical instruments, latteen (brass) candlesticks, barbers basins, cloth and other valuable goods, including the King's personal horse harness and saddles. Antonio Pacheco, a passenger, in a letter to King John later wrote that the ship was lost:–

...by reason of the great and urgent tempest of winds and weather and by the great outrages of the sea at that time chancing at Gunwalloe in the county of Cornwall. She perished and drowned in the sea there, and divers of the mariners and other persons then being in the ship were also then piteously perished and drowned.

She went ashore at 8am, having been driven by storm into a shallow bay known then as Porth Lingey, but today as Fishermen's Cove, which lies at the extreme western end of Helzepheron cliffs, in the manor of Winnianton. The lord of the manor had already sent armed retainers to the scene and taken the precaution of sending for the Helston Revenue Officer and his men to attend. He also notified William Godolphin of Breage, a Justice of the Peace in anticipation there would be fighting and disorder when the lawmen and wreckers came face to face. The Godolphins later insisted an agreement had been reached with the ship's captain regarding salvage, but the Portuguese claimed gentry and wreckers alike had robbed them!

Details of early wrecking incidents are scarce, but since the King of Portugal complained directly to King Henry VIII, the case went

Some of the brass candlesticks and candlestick fittings found on the site.

RICHARD LARN COLLECTION

to the Star Chamber whose records survive in the National Archive in London. This was the highest court in England, where alleged violence was a pre-requisite before the court would even sit in judgement. The Portuguese claimed they were forced to sell both cargo and ship, in fear of their lives. The defendants did not deny payment was made, but refused to state the amount. Agents were then sent from Antwerp to recover the cargo, but William Godolphin refused them access saying they had no letter from the King to prove ownership. By September the matter was still not resolved, and unfortunately the relevant Court Order Books disappeared during the civil wars of the 17th century, so the Court's decision remains lost. However, other evidence makes it clear the Cornish were ordered to return the goods they had stolen, or else pay their equivalent value.

In 1973 Tony Randall, an engineer at Goonhilly Satellite Earth Station was informed that an unusual copper ingot had uncovered on the beach, and he asked the author and Mike

Hall of Ruan Minor if they would dive the site? Using a special underwater metal detector, the two divers found and raised 40 'bun' shaped ingots within an hour, obviously part of the 8,000

A melon of silver found on the wreck site of the St Anthony.
RICHARD LARN COLLECTION

Some of the copper ingots located on the first dive on the wreck.
RICHARD LARN
COLLECTION

listed in the manifest. With 3,200 brass candlesticks also listed there were bound to be fragments of these left on the seabed, and by late afternoon that day dozens of candlesticks parts and their 'lion' mounting feet had been found. The most tantalising items of cargo listed were *18 cakes or blocks of silver which cost £2,250.* Was it possible some of these too might survive? Three years later Tony Randall stumbled on a solid silver 'melon' weighing 17lb (8k), a truly remarkable and unique artefact, later bought by the British Museum's Post-Medieval department for £3,500, now on public display in London.

Possibly one of the richest, if not the richest shipwreck lost on the coast of Cornwall, the *St Anthony* is now a government Protected Wreck. An interesting sideline is that the eight painted medieval wooden panels making up the historic rood screen in Gunwalloe church, and possibly those in St Budock church which escaped destruction during the Reformation, are almost certainly historic relics salvaged from this shipwreck.

Santo Christo de Castello

7 October 1667 - Polurian - Mullion

For most of the 16th century, Winnianton manor on the Lizard Peninsula was owned by the Arundell family of Lanherne, who also held title to most of the land in the Hundred of Penwith. Sir John Arundell claimed extensive right of wreck in West Cornwall, the income from which usually amounted to half the value of any wreck goods recovered, and was a jealously guarded perquisite, handed down from father to son. Mount's Bay was a fearsome trap for ships in the early days of sail, and both inward and outward bound vessels battling with prevailing southwesterly winds attempting a landfall, were equally vulnerable. Once within Mount's Bay ships frequently became 'embayed', literally trapped and unable to clear the land, blown ever closer inshore until they finally struck the coast. A 1624 letter to the Privy Council in support of a lighthouse on the Lizard Point stated:

> *Mr Cavendish endured more hazard in a storm off the Lizard than in circumnavigation of the entire globe.*

The wreck of the *Santo Christo de Castello* was found in 1969 by accident, when Peter McBride, stationed at the nearby Naval Air Station Culdrose, was exploring Meres Ledges underwater near Mullion. He came across what appeared to be iron cannons that had been sliced in half lengthwise, revealing shallow rounded troughs in which sat cannon balls! Next day back at work as stores officer at the naval base he contacted the author who worked at the Torpedo Trials Unit, relating his find and invited him to bring his boat to Mullion so they could dive together, assuming the site was a wreck. Admitting freely that he too had never seen such cannons before on the dozens of old wrecks on which he had worked, Larn realised that here was an unusual erosion situation. Lying in a shallow rock gully surrounded by deep gravel, wave action over the

One of the iron cannons from the site, showing the unusual erosion of the gun barrel, whereby half of it had been worn away by sea action.

RICHARD LARN COLLECTION

years had eaten away the iron, eroding the top half the barrel of all 23 guns to varying degrees. Loaded when the ship sank, the guns slowly wore away till the bore was exposed, leaving the iron cannon balls showing.

The divers explored the site looking for clues, returning to the boat with two important, but contrasting bits of information, one good, the other, well, noxious to say the least! Larn saw a glint of something shiny in the dense layer of concretion (hardened iron oxides) in the gravel, which was carefully dug out by hand. The object appeared to be a large silver coin or medallion, and Larn recalls his reaction as he rubbed away at one surface with a gloved finger to reveal the date MDCLIII (1653), thinking 'Good grief, that's old'! The other bit of information was that this was the most disgusting dive site in the world, since the main Mullion village sewer outfall discharged directly on top of the cannon site! Later, after chemical cleaning the 'coin' proved to be a 4.5cm diameter silver medallion bearing the legend:

Ferdinand IV nyng et boh, rex; coron; in; regem; omanorvm, VIII.IVNV. MDCLIII, whilst the obverse read *'Pro del et popvlo.*

(Ferdinand 4th, crowned King and Emperor of the Holy Roman Empire)

The wrecks identity was now paramount since a positive dating would assist a better understanding of the site and any additional finds. It was immediately obvious that his wreck did not appear in any existing wreck lists, and detailed research was necessary. For three years the site was referred to simply as the 'Mullion Pin Wreck', from the profusion of brass domestic sewing pins ranging from 3–6cms in length which littered the site in thousands, sticking through the divers' suits and gloves into knees

A magnificent pewter plate from the wreck, and a collection of domestic brass pins that littered the site in their thousands.

and hands. Its identity was discovered in the Calendar of State Papers for 1667, which recorded *'A Genoese, richly laden bound from London, after being two days at anchor, was at last cast upon the rocks and broken to pieces,'* A letter written from Pendennis Castle dated 9 October 1667 stated that:–

> *The 5th instant there was cast away neare the Lizard the Santo Christo de Castello of 56 guns and about 500 tons. A new ship built at Amsterdam and came from thence laden with iron, lead, clothes and spices to the value of £50,000 and 25 men and women drowned.*

A document found in the National Archive relating to the High Court of Admiralty (HCA30/627) had to be translated since it was written in Latin, the accepted language for all legal correspondence at the time, which read:–

> *King James II to our beloved Lord John Arundell, Francis Godolphin Esq, our Vice Admiral in the Southern parts of the County of Cornwall Colonel Lewis Tremayne Esq. Gentlemen, greetings. Concerning a certain ship called the Sanctus Christus de Castello whose captain in chief was Lorenzo Vivano and her tackle and equipment and what-ever anchors, guns and ropes belonging to the same ship and whatever goods, property, merchandise or objects of trade are found in the same about the month of October 1667 was wrecked and sunk by the force of the gale upon the shore between the growing and flowing back of the sea shall be sold to the man who offers the most, and the monies coming from their sale shall be put in the hands of the said Francis Godolphin for the use of no-one, in safe custody with a reckoning about the sale which shall be brought into the Registry of the said Court*

Divers working under McBride and Larn recovered an astonishing variety of items over the next 15 years. Despite the awful diving conditions in dilute raw sewage, toilet paper and all the unmentionables people flush down the pan, yet over all those years, none of the team was ill or suffered infection. Masks and mouth-pieces were washed in disinfectant kept on board, and on medical advice special attention was given to ear hygiene. Recoveries included lead ingots of 298lb (134 kg), musket and pistol barrels, shot, iron nails, pewter plates, religious figurines and medals, sundial 'time guns', thimbles, hundreds of fragments of brass manufactured items, and of course pins and more pins. Once a very valuable commodity subject to a special tax, pins could only be sold on certain days of the year and at certain places.

An assortment of brass artefacts from the site, including (clockwise) candlesticks, piece of the ship's bell, another pewter plate, medallion and unidentified incomplete items.

*Brass tobacco boxes and
lids, a tobacco boy and pipe,
knife sheath, a sundial time
gun miniature cannon and
religious figurines.*
RICHARD LARN COLLECTION

The wreck featured in several TV documentaries and details of their work was published in the *International Journal of Nautical Archaeology* as three long papers. One very spectacular find was a brass Tobacco Boy, a nude figure of a negro boy slave in brass 5.5ins (14cm) tall, carrying a rolled bale of tobacco leaf, his right hand holding a long 'church warden' clay smoking pipe in perfect condition. This was sold to the Imperial Tobacco Company, for display in their museum. The remains of the wreck was a success story in terms of marine archaeology, regarding discovery, research, identification, excavation, conservation, reporting and recording. the collection now on display in the Charlestown Shipwreck Heritage Centre, near St Austell.

HMS *Coronation*

3 September 1691 - Penlee - Plymouth

Built at Portsmouth Dockyard in 1685, completing the thirty year programme of warship building initiated by Admiralty Secretary Samuel Pepys, which had commenced in 1685. This included the *Coronation* and eight other 2nd rate men o'war, each armed with 90 guns, making them formidable warships.

In June 1690 the *Coronation* fought in the Battle of Beachy Head under Admiral Torrington, where the British and Dutch fleets suffered a humiliating defeat by the French, the Dutch losing 17 vessels, the British 15, the French none. This led to Torrington's imprisonment in the Tower of London, and ultimately to his court-martial and dismissal from the service. The summer of 1691 saw her with the Channel fleet at sea under Admiral Russell patrolling the French coast. In late August, a particularly severe SSW gale forced the fleet to run for Plymouth Sound, which at that time had no breakwater. The *Harwich*, *Northumberland* and *Royal Oak* struck rocks on Maker Point whilst trying to reach Devonport dockyard, and ended up ashore under Mount Edgcumbe House.

Attempting to ride out the storm outside Plymouth Sound, a number of ships anchored between Rame Head and Penlee Point, including the *Coronation*. Contemporary accounts, one written by Sir Clowdisley Shovell who was to lose his life in a shipwreck off the Isles of Scilly in 1707, stated that at 11am she lost her mainmast in heavy seas. Her crew were then seen to cut down her fore and mizzen masts, after which she capsized and disappeared some three miles offshore with the loss of over 600 men. None of the survivors left a clear account of what actually happened, and it was not until modern sport divers located first an unexplained inshore wreck site, then an offshore scatter of cannon, that the true picture emerged. A group of Plymouth divers in the 1960s found a number of large iron cannon in Lady Cove, Penlee Point, which could not be linked to any known wreck. Then in 1976 Peter McBride of Plymouth led a team of divers to locate the *Coronation* offshore. GPS (Global Positioning System) had not yet been

Peter McBride, the diver who found the offshore wreck site of the HMS Coronation *off Penlee Point in deep water, surveys one of her anchors.*

DAVID MCBRIDE

invented, so position fixing on a chart was achieved by a combination of Decca navigation equipment and two sextants, taking cross bearings of shore marks plotting exactly where the search vessel was at any one moment in time.

The work was tedious, involving hundreds of cross bearings hour after hour, with someone plotting on a navigational chart. Other team members monitored the output of a towed magnetometer, a sort of 'super' metal detector, looking for any indication of large ferrous objects such as cannon on the seabed.

The teams patience and skill paid off when they located 16 cannon in 75ft (23m) depth, whose size suggested they were upper-deck guns from a warship, but from which ship? It is remarkable that a 90 gun ship can sink yet leave few clues as to its identity. A diver has to be very lucky to establish the name of a wreck at an early stage – and both Peter McBride and his son David who were diving together, got very lucky. Trapped beneath a cannon they found a pewter plate which bore not only a crest on the rim, but the pewterer's marks on the underside. The maker proved to be James Tisoe of Westminster, who registered his touch mark in 1689, two years prior to the *Coronation* sinking. The crest proved that of the Skelton family and Charles Skelton happened to be captain of the *Coronation*! Well connected socially, he was a son of the Lieutenant Governor of Plymouth and brother to Sir Bevill Skelton, diplomat and groom of the Royal bedchamber to Charles II. The identity of the site was no longer in question.

It became obvious that after the ship capsized, allowing all her upper deck guns and anchors to fall to the seabed, including the contents of the ship's galley and captain's personal plate, she drifted inshore still upside down into Lady Cove near Penlee, where she finally broke up. Both areas of the wreck are now protected, preventing unlawful intrusion, and diving teams continue to excavate, record and research the remains.

The huge bronze bell recovered from the Coronation *site which bears only a date.*   PETER MCBRIDE

HMS *Royal Anne*

10 November 1721 - Lizard Point

Galleys, which were classed as 5th rate warships were never popular in the Royal Navy. Their combination of sail and oars were not suitable for the heavy seas and harsh northern waters of the British Isles, the design being Mediterranean where gales were infrequent and strong tides virtually unknown. Hence the navy only built six, one of which was the *Royal Anne*. Of 511-tons, she carried a crew of 247, sufficient to man her 42 guns and 60 oars or sweeps, giving this class of ship an advantage over slow or becalmed enemy vessels. Whilst described at her launch at Woolwich dockyard in1709 by the Marquis of Carmarthen as a 'new invention – the finest that ever was built', there was nothing new about such vessels, since the Romans and before them the Etruscans, had huge fleets of galleys rowed by slaves.

In November 1721, the *Royal Anne* was ordered to leave Plymouth for the West Indies specifically to take Lord Belhaven, his family, servants and retinue to Barbados where he was to take up the Governorship. This voyage was covert since the Court wished Belhaven out of the country, to avoid the scandal associated with him having murdered his wife. Any lesser mortal would have been tried and hung but men with titles were treated differently. Caught in a storm off the Lizard close inshore, when it was a long established naval practice to remain at least 18–20 leagues off, the ship was driven on to Taylors Rock where she went to pieces, drowning 244 people, only three of the crew surviving to tell the tale.

The first person to visit the wreck site was Jacob Johnson, an early Dutch diver who had invented what was described as a wooden 'dyving engine'. This was an enclosed barrel type device leaving the occupants arms protruding and free for work underwater. Alternatively, it may have been Captain Jacob Rowe, who had copied Johnson's device in sheet copper.

The site was not dived again until 1969 when students of the Bristol University Sub-Aqua Club invited Richard Larn to assist them in their survey, which revealed eight iron cannon bearing government 'broad-arrow' marks, silver coins of 1710–20 and a few items of pewter tableware, but nothing conclusive regarding identification. However, in 1992 the late 'Bob' Serrat who lived on the Lizard, dived the site and identified it as the *Royal Anne* by finding a silver spoon whose handle bore the Belhaven family crest, also gold coin and other small artefacts. The site is now a Protected Wreck.

Under charter to the Russian government, the Liverpool registered Brankelow, *ashore to the east of Loe Pool near Porthleven, 12 April 1924. The wreck was auctioned on the beach. The vessel and cargo worth £25,000 afloat was sold for just £405!*

RICHARD LARN COLLECTION

The Dollar Cove Wreck

1752 - Gunwalloe - the Lizard

A mystery wreck off the headland to the south of the church at Gunwalloe Cove, known locally as the 'Dollar Wreck', has fascinated speculators since the 1780s, many of whom went to considerable expense to find the supposed hoard of 19 tons of silver coin said to have been lost there.

In 1877, a 'Dollar Recovery Company' was formed in Helston, looking for investors to buy 200 shares at £3.00 each, to make up the required capital of £600. A John Toy, claiming to hold a Board of Trade License to search for and salvage the treasure, announced that the Company would receive £75 out of every £100 recovered. He also claimed to have researched the evidence at considerable expense, to have personally found several of the Spanish Pillar Dollars, stating that between 1784 and 1794 not one but several vessels having large quantities of dollars on board had been wrecked there. He even published a statement that up to 10 million dollars in total remained on the sea bed awaiting recovery, inviting speculators to join him. None of the 'several vessels' mentioned in the prospectus were named by John Toy, nor the identity of the supposed 'Dollar Wreck' itself.

About 1870 a shaft was sunk to 25ft(8m) in the reef at the base of the cliffs in anticipation that coins washed in by the sea would be taken up by divers. In 1872 a vicar from East London was attracted to Gunwalloe to try his luck on the basis that a summer in Cornwall would be both pleasurable and profitable, but was thwarted by bad weather and left empty handed, as have many others. The Dollar Recovery Company of 1877 set up a steam driven traction engine on the cliff, which drove via huge leather belts a suction pump set up on the rocks to pump out the shaft – and hopefully bring up coins. In 1890 when divers were working on the nearby Brankelow steamship wreck, they too dived the site but any success went unrecorded, and in 1909, a Cornish diver named Henry Rivers-Mallet brought in a floating suction dredger, but with no recorded success. The late Roland Morris of Penzance

Spanish-American silver Pillar dollars, of the type that have been found in the area of the 'Dollar Wreck' at Gunwalloe.

RICHARD LARN COLLECTION

created local headlines when he announced his plan to recover the missing treasure in the 1970s, after which a resourceful entrepreneur started hiring out metal detectors to holiday makers, inviting them to take part in a 'beach treasure hunt'. Currently, a diver from outside Cornwall has an agreement with the National Trust who own this stretch of coast, to salvage the silver. One can only wish him luck.

Legend says the wife of a Mullion man named Jeremiah Jose, dreamt she saw a bag of dollars lying on the beach. She woke her husband and begged him to go with her to visit the site but he refused, so she waited until daybreak and went down to Gunwalloe with her son. On arrival, they found a bag of dollars just as she had seen them in her dream. Struggling back up the beach with the leather bag which weighed about one hundredweight (55kg), tin miners took it from them. A fight ensued, blood was shed and the men failing to notice the incoming tide allowed the bag to became submerged and consequently lost, so that no one benefited in the end. As an aside, the spoils of the infamous pirate Captain Avery are said to be buried in the Church Cove area, even within Gunwalloe church graveyard itself, which caused the Collector of Customs for St Ives in 1770, John Knill, to apply for a Licence to dig in the area, but without success.

The truth regarding the supposed sunken treasure remains unknown, but it is unlikely that Cornish wreckers would leave 'tons' of silver coin untouched so easily accessible from the shore. There are records of 23 ships lost in the immediate area, a likely candidate being the *Fancy*, a ship of Hanover on passage from Bilbao to Amsterdam carrying cloth and a general cargo lost at Gunwalloe, November 1784. However,

TONS OF GOLD!

DANGEROUS LURE OF THE DOLLAR COVE TREASURE

Express staff reporter

An undersea hunt for one of Britain's most tantalising treasure wrecks will begin in Cornwall this summer. For 200 years a Spanish bullion carrier has lain within a stone's throw of the cliffs.

And, according to old reports, she held between three and 19 tons of gold and silver.

But ever since 1845 when the first salvage expedition went to work, the shifting sands that cover the treasure off Gunwalloe have defied all the efforts of sailors, engineers, miners and even a parish priest.

Over the years four men have died in the search for the Spanish silver. Thousands of pounds have been thrown away on ingenious or hare-brained salvage schemes.

And all the time, as if to tempt more men to financial ruin or death, a thin stream of silver dollars has been washed ashore. They have been found so regularly by beach-combers or visitors that the place is called 'Dollar Cove'.

The man that believes that the sands can at last be beaten is Mr. Roland Morris, a Penzance restaurant owner. His team of divers salvaged most of the treasure of the man-'o'war *Association*

The media love stories of sunken treasure ans attempts to recover it.
DAILY EXPRESS, JULY 1973

Lloyd's List, The Times, the Exeter Flying Post, the Sherborne & Yeovil Mercury and the Burney Collection make no mention of such a large amount of treasure lost in Cornwall. Every ship afloat carried 'ship-money' to pay the crew, for pilotage, harbour dues, stores, fuel, fresh food or water. A plausible explanation is that one or more of the known Gunwalloe wrecks carried silver Pillar Dollars for these very reasons, that a number were found at low tide whose quantity became grossly exaggerated to a ridiculous amount. The vicar of St Winwaloe church at Gunwalloe holds one such coin in trust, which the British Museum confirmed is a 'silver 8 Reales or Pillar dollar of Charles III of Spain, Potosi mint, 1784.

New bid to solve secret of sunken dollar hoard

By David Green

After his success in recovering treasure from the wreck of HMS *Association*, off the Isles of Scilly, Mr Roland Morris is to join the ranks of the "Dollar Men", the treasure seekers, whose often ingenious attempts to salvage the valuable cargo of a sunken Spanish ship at the mouth of Gunwalloe Cove have so far failed.

Mr. Morris, the proprietor of a Penzance restaurant, admitted yesterday that he was not very hopeful of success. "We know where the wreck is but recovering any of the treasure will be extremely difficult.

The ship, it's identity is uncertain, sank in about 1787, with a hoarde of silver dollars, allegedly up to 19 tons of the coins. The main problem which Mr. Morris and the team of divers must overcome is shifting sand. "It can shift daily and we will have to wait for just the rght diving conditions", he said.

A recent survey he made of the area showed that the wreck was covered by 12 ft. of sand. "We hope to start work in October", he explained, which is usually the best month for diving." Salvage attempts would take up to three years.

"I want to have a go, become a "Dollar Man" whether or not I am successful.

He claimed even if the treasure were recovered, it would not be worth "all that much". The coins would have stuck together and the outer ones damaged.

If his divers cannot recover the treasure, Mr. Morris continued, he might seek permission to build scaffoldding from Castle Mount on the shore in another attempt to reach it.

He was also interested in a nearby wreck of an East Indiaman.

The late Roland Morris of Penzance made much of his attempt to locate the Dollar Wreck in the media, but confided to friends he was not hopeful.

Transport *Dispatch* & HMS *Primrose*

22 January 1809 - the Manacles

The most notorious and feared navigational hazard on the south coast of Cornwall is the Manacles reef, which covers some one and a half square miles to the south of Falmouth. The names of over a hundred and twenty ships are recorded that have been lost here, the number of lives in excess of a thousand, its evil reputation reflected in its sinister name. With deep water right up to its outer eastern face, which instantly changes to shallow reef and sharp rocks, it has claimed full-rigged ships, a man o'war, sailing coasters, steamships and even a liner, which lost 106 passengers and crew.

January 1809 saw a small British army under General Sir John Moore retreating across the mountains of northern Spain, hotly pursued by a vastly superior French force commanded by Napoleon Bonaparte. Both men and pack animals were in an appalling condition, more from the unaccustomed cold and continuous rain than physical combat. Day after day they retreated, eventually reaching Corunna, where Admiralty hired transport vessels were waiting. The 7th Dragoons, much depleted in men and horses boarded the *Dispatch*, Captain Barclay, taking on all that remained of a fine regiment, just three officers, seventy-two men and thirty-six horses. Dodging gunfire from French batteries high above the harbour, they sailed for Plymouth on 14 January, but eight days later encountered snow and a gale that reached hurricane force. At 3.30am on Sunday 22nd the transport drove ashore near Lowlands Point, between Coverack and Porthoustock, inside of the Manacles. It was impossible to launch a boat from either ship or shore, and In total darkness the *Dispatch* went to pieces, surrounded by huge seas and fearful rocks which tore men and animals to pieces. Daybreak revealed mutilated bodies washing about in the shallows, with only seven survivors. Amongst the dead were Major Cavendish, the 25 years old son of Lord Cavendish, also Lieutenant the Hon Edward Waldgrove, 3rd son of the 4th Earl of Waldgrove. The dead remained uniden-tified until fellow officers from another transport, the *Barfleur* reached Plymouth, and on hearing the news travelled to St Keverne church where the bodies were laid out.

The night the *Dispatch* was lost saw another wreck at the north end of the Manacles, prompting six Porthoustock fishermen to put to sea. George and Edward Tonkin, Stephen Old, Bartholomew Tripp, William Matthews and his brother Joseph, manned the largest boat they owned and rowed out into the night. Hours later, soaked and exhausted they returned with the sole survivor of the wreck, a ten year old ship's boy named John Meaghen. He related that the ship was the 18-gun brig-o'war HMS *Primrose,* outward bound for Corunna under Commander James Mein RN, which had struck the reef at 5am whilst carrying 126 officers and seamen, plus six passengers. Interestingly, she was Cornish built having been launched at Fowey only the previous year.

At least 270 people died in the two wrecks, of which only

110 bodies were recovered, 104 being buried in St Keverne churchyard between 24 January and 2 April. A large memorial tablet placed on the wall inside the church was donated by fellow officers of the regiment, which for some reason was removed in later years, finding its way into a large private house near Helston. Remaining in the church is a marble plaque holding a brass gudgeon or rudder fitting from the Primrose. The warship sank in the vicinity of Carn Du, where, in 1965, a small brass signal or saluting gun was found by a diver, now on public display in the Charlestown Shipwreck Centre. The graves of the victims are marked with headstones in St. Keverne churchyard, and an iron 32 pounder carronade gun from the *Primrose* stands on the surrounding wall near the gated entrance, one of four recovered in recent years by divers.

A 32 pounder carronade gun from HM brig Primrose, *mounted on a replica gun slide outside St Keverne church, where many of the victims were buried.*

RICHARD LARN COLLECTION

Emigrant Ship *John*

3 May 1855 - the Manacles

No doubt the older residents of Porthallow, Porthoustock and St. Keverne were still reminiscing over the loss of the *Dispatch* and *Primrose* in 1809 when in 1855 there was an equally disastrous wreck involving an emigrant ship. When finally a full account of this tragic event was made public in the *Royal Cornwall Gazette* and other local newspapers, people were initially unable to believe it was true – that men could treat others with such total disregard, inhumanity and callous behaviour.

The Plymouth registered barque *John* of 486-tons, spent the early 1850s transporting emigrants to Canada and the United States without incident. In early 1855 she underwent a complete overhaul, the docking, scraping, painting and new rigging costing the owners £200. Advertisements offered passage to Quebec sailing on 3 May, but workmen were still completing jobs as the first emigrants walked up the gangway. She left Plymouth at 4pm on schedule under the command of Captain Edward Rawle, having 149 adults, 98 children, 16 babies and 16 crew, a total of 279 men and women, who waved farewell to friends and relatives as they left the dockside. With a NW wind she soon cleared the Sound, then set sail for the run down the English Channel. At 9.30pm the St Anthony lighthouse was sighted followed by the lights of Falmouth town, which the captain pointed out to several passengers. When the Lizard light failed to show the mate advised the captain who retorted, 'You'll see it soon enough when we get there', and retired to his cabin. The Lizard had still not been sighted an hour later, by which time the wind had increased pushing the *John* closer to shore. Breakers were then reported ahead by the lookout, and almost simultaneously she struck the Manacles. Her inertia, assisted by a huge swell carried her over the outer rocks where the crew dropped an anchor but she continued to drive, finishing up on to the rocks near Lowlands Point.

The ship carried four lifeboats, three on their chocks, one slung outboard level with the main deck for emergencies. No sooner had the ship come to a complete stop than the captain, four crew and a wealthy passenger climbed in, saying they were going for help. Despite the refit in Plymouth, the boat was in a shocking state, no plug for the bung-hole and neither rowlocks or thole pins to use with the oars. The hole was plugged with a twist of cloth, marlin-spikes improvised as thole-pins and it's a wonder the boat ever reached Coverack. Following the captain's example, some of the male passengers tried to launch one of the other boats, but it smashed against the barque's side and sank. The crew, apart from the steward, did nothing to help, climbing into the rigging carrying bottles of drink they had pilfered from the spirit store, and proceeded to get drunk. On the flood tide heavy seas commenced to break over the ship, forcing the

Artefacts recovered from the wreck of the John, *(L to R) wooden deadeye; lead scupper pipe and 'lead through' for a rigging rope.*

passengers into the rigging, only to be beaten back by the crew. One young couple tied their two infants into a bed sheet and hoisted it into the rigging, but either a wave caught it or the cloth tore, since it fell overboard and the children drowned. Huge waves now swept the deck from bow to stern, hurling men and women against the bulwarks, breaking limbs or washing them overboard. Despite being May, it was bitterly cold and the women in the lower rigging, unable to retain a handhold, dropped into the sea one by one.

It was daybreak before the sea subsided sufficiently for the Coverack Coastguard boat to be launched, after which the Porthoustock lifeboat arrived alongside. Three trips to Coverack by the two boats saved 70 men and women, but 193 had died during the night. Even when it was obvious that everyone would be taken off safely, the crew fought the passengers for places in the boats. They were later described by the media as 'a drink-smelling rabble', and not one of the crew lost their possessions, let alone a life. At the resultant Inquest and subsequent Board of Trade enquiry, the captain and his entire crew (apart from the steward) were condemned for their callous behaviour. The enquiry revealed the ship carried no distress flares, rockets or signal guns, and that not one of her lifeboats was seaworthy. A verdict of manslaughter was returned against the captain, who was arrested and thrown into Bodmin gaol awaiting trial. He later received a prison sentence, as did a number of St Keverne men who were caught looting from the dead as they lay amongst the rocks. A memorial tablet in St Keverne church reads,

Sacred to the memory of 120 people here interred,
who were drowned in the wreck of the John, *3 May 1855.*
Erected by the survivors.

ss *Czar*

22 January 1859 - Vrouge Rock, the Lizard

The very first steamship wrecked on the Lizard was the Liverpool registered *Zebra* of 435-tons net, on passage from Le Havre to her homeport with cotton and manufactured goods, plus 28 passengers. In dense fog and off course, she drove into Parnvoose Cove at Bass Point on 22 July 1856. No lives were lost and like many wrecks there was no real story, unlike the next steamer wreck on the Lizard, which occurred on 22 January 1859.

Samuelson & Son built the 1,100-ton barque rigged ss.*Czar* at Kingston-upon-Hull in 1858, which carried a crew of 28 under Captain Jackson. In 1859 she was hired by the British government to carry military stores to the garrison at Malta, which required her to enter the Thames and berth at Woolwich arsenal. Here, huge wooden sheer legs acting as a crane carefully lowered 51 enormous 68-pounder Lancaster muzzle-loading guns into her hold, each weighing in the order of 10 tons. In addition she took on board hundreds of cast-iron round shot for the guns, plus uniform clothing, hides, spirits, oil, sugar and cinnamon, a total dead weight of 1,600 tons. On sailing she successfully cleared the Downs and English Channel in rough blustery weather, but ran into a full gale 50 miles west of the Isles of Scilly. Rolling heavily carrying such a dead weight cargo, she developed problems with both boilers, and was forced to turn back for Falmouth for repairs, but never got that far. By early afternoon of 22 January in worsening weather, the *Czar* was close inshore, her captain at the wheel, seeking shelter of the high cliffs east of the Lizard where she struck the Vrogue Rock. Badly holed and rapidly filling with water, she fell beam on to heavy seas which caused her to roll until her lower yards touched the sea, at which point she broke in two, both halves sinking as they drifted apart.

Two seamen and a male passenger were swept off the forecastle into a heaving sea, followed shortly after by the occupants of one of her two boats which capsized. The second boat managed to reach the shore with just three survivors on board, who advised the Lizard Coastguards of the wreck, who put out in a cutter. With only three men saved from the rigging and another found swimming in the sea, a total of seventeen crew lost their lives along with all three passengers. Captain Jackson drowned in the cabin trying to reach his wife and five-year-old son when the ship broke in two, the bodies all being buried in Landewednack churchyard on the Lizard.

The Hull registered freeze trawler Conqueror *swept ashore near Penzer Point, Mousehole 26 December 1977.* GIBSONS OF SCILLY

Jonkheer Meester Van de Wall

26 March 1867 - Poldew Cove

All the crew except one of the *Jonkheer Meester Van de Wall de Puttershoek*, to give this Dutch East Indiaman its full name, as well as the seven passengers, died unseen and in total darkness when she drove ashore under Angrouse cliffs, near Poldhu Cove on the Lizard. Commanded by Captain Klass Lammerts, carrying a crew of nineteen and passengers, the thirteen year-old ship was 140 days out from Batavia for Amsterdam carrying coffee, sugar, arrowroot and tin ingots worth £50,000 when lost. A Mousehole pilot boat had seen her tacking back and forth between the Lizard and Mullion, but declined to offer their services having recently received poor treatment from foreign ships; and in any case this vessel did not seem to be in any distress, so they let it pass.

Nothing more of the vessel was seen until 2am on the 26th March when Mullion coastguards saw distress rockets climb into the sky, and an hour later coastguards found wreckage around Poldhu Cove. Dawn revealed the entire poop of a barque, the bodies of two women, aged about 25 and 40, a three-day-old baby and several sailors. Then a bedraggled survivor was found stumbling amongst the rocks who was taken to Mullion vicarage in the hope that the Reverend Harvey, something of a linguist, could interrogate him since the man spoke no English. He proved to be Georgio Buffani, a Greek sailor, who had joined the ship in Batavia, but was unsure of the name of his ship or her captain! From a list of East Indiamen he picked out the name *Kosmopoliet*, but shortly after the inquest two Dutch sea captains in Falmouth expressed the opinion she was the *Jonkheer Meester*. Proof was forthcoming when a Masonic diploma for Captain Lammert was found washed ashore. Recovered from the wreck were 850 tons of coffee, the sugar in bamboo baskets, a box containing gold coins, banknotes and feminine jewellery, and the tin. Later, a will, identifying one of the dead women as a governess retiring after years in India, was found in the shattered poop deck wreckage whilst being dismantled.

This brand-new five-masted German schooner Adolf Vinnen *was swept ashore near Bass Point on the Lizard on 23 February 1924. The captain, officers and a steward remained on board, they were saved the next day when heavy seas swept over the deck and they were forced to cling to the rigging.* Richard Larn Collection

Full rigged ship
Bay of Panama

10 March 1891 - Porthallow

A legend in Cornwall's maritime history, this four-masted, square-rigged steel ship was a victim of the Great Blizzard of 1891. Built by Harland & Wolff at Belfast in 1883, along with the *Cutty Sark* she was described as amongst the finest sailing ships ever built. She had left Calcutta on 18 November 1890 with 13,000 bales of jute for the mills at Dundee. On reaching the approach to the English Channel, Captain David Wright became concerned by signs of an approaching blizzard, which later proved to be the worst the West Country had known for 200 years.

A little after 1.30am on 10 March a huge wave overtook the ship, sweeping from stern to bow, destroying every boat on deck. Shortly after, still in driving snow, nil visibility and hurricane force easterly winds, she plunged headlong into the cliffs south of Nare Point, in Porthallow Bay. She was only seven miles from the safety of Falmouth harbour, having travelled half way round the world, almost 12,000 miles. One mast collapsed immediately, then both fore and main topmasts broke off and fell into the sea in a tangle of rigging. The 2nd Mate had no sooner fired a distress rocket than a wave washed him overboard where he drowned. The same wave demolished the cabin, sweeping the captain, his wife, cook, steward and four young apprentices overboard into the sea. The remaining crew took to the rigging, except for the carpenter and sail maker who left it too late and they too were washed overboard.

With the temperature well below freezing, the extreme cold and exposure soon took its toll. The bosun went out of his mind and leapt into the sea, and at least six seamen literally froze to death where they clung. A local farmer found the ship, less than 50ft from the rocks; a breeches buoy was rigged and just seventeen survivors from her crew of forty were brought ashore. Deep snowdrifts blocked the road and they were forced to walk the rest of the way, some without socks or shoes. A *Falmouth Packet* reporter commented, 'they endured as much privation in that walk as they did in the actual shipwreck.'

The battered wreck of the Bay of Panama *after being driven ashore in a blizzard close to Porthallow.*

Full-rigged ship
Andola

29 January 1895 - Shark's Fin, Manacles

This Liverpool registered ship left England in 1893 with a cargo of coke for the copper mines of California. In 1894 she sailed for Seattle, discharged her stone ballast and and was towed to Elliott Bay where she loaded 2,000 tons of grain. Due to a series of gales, took a phenomenal one hundred and eighty days for her to cross the Atlantic, and she was more than two months overdue when she finally limped into Falmouth Roads. That same day her owners ordered Captain Passmore to sail immediately for Hull to discharge, a harsh order after their privations of six months at sea. She left on the evening tide and within an hour was off the Eddystone, but a change of wind forced the *Andola* to tack right across the Channel until they saw the lights of France, then back until they saw the Lizard light.

The ship was now being driven steadily backwards by wind and tide, then a snow storm reduced visibility to a few yards, during which an apprentice reported he could hear a bell clanging to seaward. When the snow cleared, they found themselves well inside of the Manacles buoy and in serious trouble. Without warning at about 8pm in the dark, the ship drove into the Shark's Fin Rock, just a stones throw from Porthoustock beach. The same apprentice that had reported the bell was sent to fetch flares from the chartroom but these proved damp, and failed to ignite. He then went below to fetch 'bomb-rockets' from the magazine, but sparks from the sputtering flare he carried fell amongst the rockets setting them off. One burst up through the upper deck, shrapnel flinging the lad unconscious into the scuppers, another blew the roof off the charthouse, injuring the helmsman. The explosions were so loud they brought out the Falmouth lifeboat on the rumour a liner was aground! Any grain cargo swells rapidly when wet, and in this instance the upper deck bulged, then split, whilst several side plates actually burst open as she became a total wreck.

There is a model of the *Andola* on display in the Five Pilchard's pub at Porthallow, along with a large brass letter 'A' from the name on her bow.

The wreck of the Andola *near the Manacles, Porthoustock, with her bowsprit almost touching the Shark's Fin Rock.*

GIBSONS OF SCILLY

ss *Mohegan*

14 October 1898 - the Manacles

S ailors at one time firmly believed it was bad luck to change a ship's name. This hardly applies today when ships may have as many as eight or nine name changes, but when the liner *Cleopatra* became the *Mohegan* following her maiden voyage, there was a degree of unrest amongst her crew. Built for the Wilson Furness Leyland Line by Earles of Hull, prior to launching she was purchased by the Atlantic Transport Co who announced the intended name change. Her bad luck seemingly started immediately when a strike held up her completion, and unfinished when she sailed, she leaked so badly she had to be dry docked the moment she reached New York.

Her maiden voyage completed, she was dry-docked on the Tyne where the leaks were stopped and essential repairs carried out, at which point she was re-named. On 13 October 1898 she sailed on her 2nd voyage under Captain Griffiths, commodore of the line, carrying 57 passengers, 100 crew and seven cattlemen. Her cargo included beer and spirits, lead, antimony, artificial flowers, church ornaments, glass and seed. As she passed Rame Head, Plymouth, she was ten miles offshore and why she did not maintain this distance down to the Lizard is a mystery. Four people saw the *Mohegan* during the last minutes of her existence, boatmen Snell of the Falmouth coastguards, the Receiver of Wrecks, a Mr. Fooks, James Hill, coxswain of the Porthoustock lifeboat, and Charlie

May, a Coverack coastguard. All saw her lights as she neared the Manacles, and each, instinctively, knew she was heading into danger. Coxswain Hill was the most intuitive, calling out his lifeboat crew and getting the boat afloat before the liner even struck the rocks. His prompt action was the saving of many lives, which otherwise would have been lost.

The passengers on board were just sitting down to dinner, the ship steaming at full speed when, at about 6.50pm, the vessel shuddered and came to a graceful stop. With a huge gash in her starboard side from hitting the Voices rocks, she quickly flooded and assumed a 40° list which rendered her starboard boats useless. The Porthoustock lifeboat reached the scene saving two men on an upturned lifeboat, then dragged two women and a dead child from beneath another that had been trapped there for over an hour. When the magnitude of the disaster was realised, lifeboats from Falmouth, Cadgwith, Coverack and the Lizard were all launched to assist. Of the

Built as the ss *Cleopatra her name was changed to* Mohegan; *she was on her second passage to the USA when she was wrecked off the Manacles.*

Lifebelts, cork lifejackets, gratings and wood washed ashore at Porthoustock following the loss of the liner.

The mass grave of victims from the wreck of the Mohegan, *prepared in St Keverne churchyard. The coffins are already two deep and a third layer is yet to be added.*

liners 100 crew only 38 were saved, and 13 of the 57 passengers, the death toll being 106. Most of the dead were interred in a mass grave on the north side of the churchyard at St Keverne, others were embalmed and sent to America, the company paying the passage of relatives who wished to visit the grave, marked today with a plain tall granite cross. A headless corpse washed ashore in Caernarvon Bay, Wales, some months later, was dressed in a sea captain's uniform with buttons embossed 'ATL', which left little doubt that these were the remains of Captain Griffiths.

This photograph supposedly shows the Porthoustock lifeboat Charlotte *saving passengers and crew from the rigging of the* Mohegan, *but it is posed, since her funnel showed for 10 days after the wreck.*

ROYAL INSTITUTE OF CORNWALL

Schooner
Capitaine Remy

29 November 1920 - St.Austell Bay

The first intimation the authorities had that this Bordeaux registered auxiliary screw, five-masted schooner was in trouble, was the arrival back at Brixham of the fishing smack *Vigilant* with 38 French survivors on board. The smack was returning from the Bristol Channel fishing grounds when, some 14 miles off the Lizard in a gale she spotted distress signals. She closed on a vessel sunk so low that the upper deck was awash, her crew in three boats attached to the stern. By the time the crew had been rescued the wreck had drifted to within eight miles of the Lizard, and the smack left for Brixham assuming it would sink.

Meanwhile Falmouth Coastguards' were receiving various reports from vessels concerning a derelict schooner adrift in the Channel, which was a serious navigational hazard to shipping. The next sighting reported a large vessel capsized and bottom up 8 miles SE of the Lizard, which was initially thought to be the ss *Burnside*. She had been towed in from off the Isles of Scilly having been on fire and abandoned, then moored temporarily in Gerrans Bay. The ss *Marena* then reported finding the derelict along with three small boats containing the ship's papers of a French vessel, the *Capitaine Remy*, a 2,114-ton ship carrying coal from Barry to Nantes.

For days the elusive derelict drifted around the Channel, sighted one day then lost the next, until it turned up off Pentewan, near Black Head. Falmouth tugs took it in tow and brought it into St Austell Bay, where she was moored, upside down, off Polkerris, awaiting disposal.

Divers removed her broken masts and rigging, in the hope she could be righted, but she refused to turn over despite every effort. She was finally stripped of all non-ferrous items, which included her propeller, shafting, rudder hangings and intake connections. She was then towed into Fowey where the lower part of her frames and keel are still used as a docking 'grid' by fishing craft opposite the china clay jetties.

The upturned hull of the five-masted schooner Capitaine Remy, *after being towed into Porthkerris Bay, St Austell Bay, having capsized out in the English Channel.*

Submarines

1921 - offshore and Gyllyngvase - Falmouth

At the end of WWI a total of 105 German U-boat submarines which had surrendered to the Allies, were allotted to the Royal Navy as war reparations. These were put to various uses, some towed to seaports and opened to the public, who could go on board and see for themselves the nature of these enemy warships that had created such havoc amongst our merchant vessels. Others were used as targets for naval weapons trials, others simply broken up for their scrap metal value, which was considerable, remembering that most of their torpedo tubes were bronze. Nine of these surrendered submarines were allocated to Falmouth for gunnery trials, two of which were sunk in the bay soon after arrival. Another, UB-118, never reached Falmouth, having parted her tow off Dodman Point where she was sunk by gunfire from the armed fishery protection trawler HMS *Kennet*. The remaining six U-boats were moored at Gyllyngvase, but a severe winter storm parted their anchors allowing one to go ashore on the beach, the others stranding on rocks below Pendennis Castle Point.

These became an instant tourist attraction, and local boatmen ferried people out from the town to see them, telling lurid stories regarding the death and destruction they had achieved when in service. The submarines were the UB-86; UB-97; UB-106; UB-112; UB-128 and UC-92. The stranded hulks lay in the shallows, some partially exposed at low water right through until WW2, when scrap metal greatly increased in value, and they were salvaged. Today, they are still a tourist attraction, only now it is underwater tourism, and sport divers still find them extremely interesting.

Fifteen miles south of Falmouth lies another submarine attracting the attention of deep divers This is the wreck of HM submarine *Narwhal,* one of the Porpoise class built by Vickers, the first to spend a month beneath the Arctic ice cap in 1963. Obsolete and surplus to requirements, she was sunk in Weymouth Bay in 1980 as part of a NATO submarine SUBSMASH salvage exercise, then having been raised, she was scuttled off Falmouth on 3 August 1983 as a sonar training target.

During salvage work during WW2, the submarines were cut up and sections dragged ashore on the rocks.

RICHARD LARN COLLECTION